Dalesfolk and Dialect

In this series:
THE FABULOUS CLIFFORDS
REGINALD FARRER
KIT CALVERT: YORKSHIRE DALESMAN

Dalesfolk and Dialect

W R Mitchell

CASTLEBERG
2003

For

ALISON BOOTHMAN

A **Castleberg** Book

First published in the United Kingdom in 2003

Copyright © W R Mitchell 2003

The moral right of the author has been asserted

ISBN 1 871064 33 3

Typeset in Giovanni, printed and bound in the
United Kingdom by Lamberts Printers,
Station Road, Settle, North Yorkshire, BD24 9AA

Published by Castleberg, 18 Yealand Avenue, Giggleswick,
Settle, North Yorkshire, BD24 0AY

Contents

Yorkshire Speech	7
Native Expressions	12
Mother Tongue	15
Written Words	20
Yorkshire Types	23
A Smattering of Dialect	26
A Funny County	28
Some Yorkshire Speyks	30
An Assortment of Similies	33
Mythical Celebrities	35
Dale and Fell	36
Wild Nature	39
Weather Lore	41
The Farming Scene	43
In the Home	49
Food and Drink	52
Human Affairs	56
Not so Weal	60
Improving	63
Last Legs	64
Glossary	67
Tale End	72

Acknowledgements

THIS introduction to Yorkshire dialect was compiled during research for a short course on Heritage Studies organised by the Craven College for Settle Court House. The author's special insight into folk-speech came through his editorship of *The Dalesman* over many years, his friendship with such as Kit Calvert, J R Gregson and Sam Dyson and his residence in Austwick – "cuckoo town" – half a century ago. A booklet of great reference value is *A Bonny Hubbleshoo* (1970), by Margaret Batty, who deals with folk-speech she recorded in Swaledale. Two modern classics, compiled by Arnold Kellett, are *The Yorkshire Dictionary of Dialect, Tradition and Folklore* (1994) and *Basic Broad Yorkshire* (1991). Arnold was for many years editor of the *Transactions* of the Yorkshire Dialect Society.

Illustrations

Cover photography by W R Mitchell. Line drawings by Richard Bancroft.

YORKSHIRE SPEECH

REET, then! Just remember tha's in York*sher*, not York*shire*. And that just as anyone born and bred in Yorkshire doesn't chuck hard-earned brass about, so there's no need to use two words where one'll do. When a Leeds telemarketing company – whatever that is – announced it was looking for the authentic voice of Yorkshire, there were titters. We have dozens of authentic Yorkshire voices, as you'd find if you were to go for a long car ride. Stop every few miles and ask the way. You'll be fair capped [astonished, surprised, sore amazed] at the variety.

Yorkshire is England's greatest county, judging by its size. An American stationed among the radomes on Menwith Hill, near Harrogate, said Yorkshire is the Texas of England. "And you sure brag about it." Whatever happens, we don't waste words. The classic business conversation, between a shopkeeper and a commercial traveller, runs like this: "Mornin'." "Owt?" "Nowt." "Mornin'."

I've already mentioned money. In Yorkshire you *addle* [earn] it. If you are setting off you are *getting agate*. Use *allus* for always and *summat* for something. The word *middlin'*, meaning moderate, and applied almost exclusively to a state of health, has fine shades of meaning. The definition of a bore is one who, when asked about his/her health, goes into full details. A taciturn Yorkshire tyke replied, somewhat vaguely: "Nay, I doubt I'm nobbut just middlin'." A bow-legged chap *couldn't stop a pig in a ginnel* [narrow passage].

Arthur Raistrick, the Dales antiquary, in a reference to dialect poetry, observed that it is dear to the heart of the people in a way that "literature" never is or can be. It is concerned with the events of everyday life – with little events, experiences, humour, sympathies and emotions of very ordinary people. Prime examples of native poetry are the works of Tommy Blackah, a lead-miner on Greenhow Hill, and Tom Twistleton, a Settle blacksmith, who in 1867 introduced a small collection of poems in dialect:

> *Good reader, when ye tack a look*
> *Within the leaves of this lile book,*

Ye needn't stare and wonder,
If, when across its lines ye glance,
Ye pop upon a word by chance
    That seems to be a blunder.

For we who speak this dialect,
To grammar fine an' words correct
    We hev but sma' pretence;
An' when our speeches, rough an' queer,
Fa' on a finely-polished ear,
    'Twill hardly sound like sense.

Kit Calvert, of Hawes, translated passages from The Bible into the dialect of his native Wensleydale. When someone condemned him for treating the Holy Word thus, Kit remarked: "Christ spoke in a dialect." I like Kit's handling of the classic English rendering of St Luke's Gospel, chapter fifteen, and especially: "Noo, awl t'taxgitherers an' knockaboots crooded roond ta hear Him, an' t'Pharasees an' t'lawyers chuntered and said, 'This feller tek's up wi' good-fer-nowts an' eyts wi' 'em'."

Also enjoyable was the dialect-laden speech of Susan Peacock, who in the 1930s ran Tan Hill Inn, at

1,732 ft the highest pub in the land. Its remoteness had an appeal for visitors. They latched on to every word uttered by Susan. Asked if she went to church, she remarked: "No, I doesn't – but I respects those at do." She had been to a broadcasting studio in Leeds with the Swaledale Singers and, naturally, was asked for her views on radio. She said: "A few folks bring t'wireless up to Tan Hill wi' 'em in their cars. I've soon hed enuff of it. Michael [her husband] isn't struck on it either."

Brig. A bridge.

Practice basic West Riding dialect by reciting *Ilkla Moor*. Take a hammer and flatten your vowels. You'll have to do this up t'dales, especially if you are crossing from Wensleydale to Swaledale by the Buttertubs Pass. This should never be pronounced Battertabs, which some posh visitors say. The poems of John Thwaite, of Wensleydale, offer a good introduction to Dales dialect, especially his account of a hayfield attack by midges, from which I cull these lines: "Neea shakkin' off, neea good te pleean,/They help thersels te fat an' lean."

Crack a joke. Especially one about sheep or wool. An impatient motorist who was following a flock of sheep along a narrow road, saw they were attended by several frustrated men and dogs. The motorist wound down the window of his car and asked who was the master of the flock. An exasperated farmer replied: "Yon lile black-faced 'un at t'front."

Native Expressions

THROUGHOUT my life, I have been surrounded by the homely wash of Yorkshire speech, much of it in dialect. If someone said *sitha* it was a command to look. If the weather was about to *tak-up*, it would brighten. Anyone who complained was *chuntering*. If they trifled with something they were *faffing*. A quarrelsome couple were *fratching*. After a meal, I might help to *side the pots away*. To be *near* implied stinginess and *scratting* – from the Danish kratte, to scratch – was being finnicky. A *sackless* person was lazy. And if you were *brazzened* you had no sense of shame.

My paternal Grannie, as Yorksher as they mak' em, and a source of many native expressions, had started life as a mill town lass, walking across the dale in clogs to her employment. Yet she lived well into her nineties. When she tumbled for the umpteenth time, she remarked: "If owt else happens to me – tha mun shoot me."

Grannie was a Methodist, having a faith that was

simple but strong. Methodism came to dominate the religious life of the northern dales, where the dialect was robust, as evidenced by the man who, having suffered misfortune, offered this prayer: "O Lord, thoo's tried ma in sorrow, thoo's tried ma in affliction an' thoo's tried ma in poverty. Next time, if it be thy will, just try ma wi' a bit o' brass."

He who was distended with good eating was *brussened*. This might happen at a communal tea held at t'chapil. It was called a Faith Tea until someone remarked: "I've more faith than t'lot on you. I've browt nowt." Then it became a Jacob's Join, though no one could satisfactory explain how Jacob had become involved. In Grannie's frugal world, you might *suffer a backening*, which meant you had been retarded or put back. If you were busy, then you were *throng*. The person who was even busier was *fair backset and foreset*.

Grannie called a child a *bairn* and a length of string was *band*. Her old age led to a temporary memory loss; but then she *bethowt* herself and her train of thought could be completed. A chap who had a good line in nonsense was a *blether'eead*. The dialect I heard as a lad was expressive, as evidenced by a description of a lass with straight hair – *that it stuck out like peggy feet.* Peggy was an implement used in a tub on wash-day. A housewife cramped for space at home *wor proper thrussen.*

Batch. To beat up an egg.

Mother Tongue

OUR Yorkshire dialect can be traced to the speech of land-hungry tribes from Europe who, in the fifth century, crossed the North Sea for a landfall on the north-east coast. Their language has been described as "a kind of cross between German and Geordie". The invaders encountered a scattering of Celtic folk, with whom they could not converse. The Celtic folk were pushed to the far west. The Anglians retained a few of their terms for natural features, especially rivers, which to the Celts were sacred places. The root name for Aire and Ure was *isara* [strong] and Nidd may have been derived from *nei* [shining]. They had named one hill Penyghent and a lesser hill they knew as Chevin. The Celts were almost certainly the first people to define the area that was to become Yorkshire. To them it was Deira – land of the brave.

A curious set of sheep-counting numerals, said to hark back to Celtic times, ran to twenty, at which stage the shepherd might slip a stone from one pocket to another and start again. One form runs: *Yan, tan, tether, pathas, pimp, setha, letha, hova, dova, dik; yan-a-dik, tan-a-dik, tethra-dick, petha-dik, bomfit, yan-a-bomfit, tan-a-bomfit, teth-a-bomfit, path-a-bomfit, gigit.* We are beholden to the Celtic folk for the term *Mam*. Their *Tad* became Dad. The Yorkshire flair for both making and retaining *brass* [money] possibily sprang from Celtic times, where the word *cael* meant acquisition, leading to "He'll cowl it in reight enuff". *Kysty*, which means faddy about food, has its root in *cysetlyd*, the Celtic word for fastidious.

Angles arriving on the east coast claimed the area lying east of the Pennines and twixt Humber and Forth, hence Northumbria. The river Wharfe was a likely boundary between two Anglian kingdoms, those of Northumbria and Mercia. The everyday speech of Mercians who moved northwards into what became the West Riding was harsher than that of the north and east.

Subsequent invaders, of Danish stock, known as Vikings, after the *viks* or creeks from which they had sailed, had a language that differed in some respects from that of the Angles but had enough in common for them to become amalgamated into a common speech. The old Yorkshire dialect was heavily laden with Danish words. Arthur Raistrick, Dales antiquary, claimed that anyone with a quick ear and a good knowledge of the Yorkshire dialects, along with some Danish, would find many close similarities not only in vocabulary but in grammar and construction.

The Norwegians (Norsemen) who arrived in the western dales of Yorkshire should more properly be known as Irish-Norse. Some of those who sailed around the top of Scotland, then southwards, founded a Viking kingdom around Dublin in the late 9th century. At the beginning of the following century, they were raiding the western coastline of Britain and settling in the north-west. Norse place-names are known from the suffixes *thwaite, thorpe* and *bye*. The word dale was derived from the Norse *dalr* for valley. Other common Norse words include *gill* for water-carved valley and *tarn* for a small lake, *addle* for earn and *agate* for busy.

The extent of the Norse colonisation can be roughly traced on a map by reference to the *fells*, which was the Norse name for hill. The Danes gave us *carrs, riggs, gaits, dykes* and *ings*. Their word *ligge*, to lie, is evident in the command: "Lig thi dahn, lad." The Danish word *bagende*, meaning hind-part, is perpetuated in the term back-end, which became a commonplace of everyday speech. The Scandinavian settlers, with their flair for administration, divided the county into three parts, the *thriddings*, which in time became Ridings.

Norman invaders, speaking French, had little effect on Yorkshire dialect. The Norman aristocracy was a class apart and the next option to French was Latin. William the Conqueror, facing an Anglo-Danish revolt in which three thousand of the Norman garrison of York were slain, swore to take vengeance on local folk and did so in the severe winter of 1069-70 with what became known as the "harrying" of the North. Hence a Yorkshire expression "swearing like Billyo."

Few ordinary folk were literate. Dialects were a matter of everyday speech until the latter part of the fifteenth century when English became standardised. A century before, Ranulph Higden, a southerner, wrote: "Alle the languages of the Northumbres and specially at York is so sharp, slyting frotying and unshape that we sothern men may unneth understande that language."

Faad. A sheep fold.

WRITTEN WORDS

YORKSHIRE dialect is variable but might be split into three blocs – North, East and (distinctively) West. Differences in dialect are evidenced by the word "about" which, when spoken in the north and east, becomes a cooing sound, *aboot*, whereas the West Riding pronunciation is the coarser *abaht*. The softer speech of the east meant that *how* became *hoo*. This could be confusing, as when a visitor asked a native "and who are you?" The reply was: "Aw – nobbut middlin'. Hoo's yoursen?"

A poem about a Wensleydale lad's visit to Leeds and his first entry into a church were recorded in verse. He saw "thirty or forty folk, i' tubs an' boxes sat, when up cooms a saucy owd fellow, who said: "Noo lad, tak off thi hat.". When the preachin' an' prayin' were over, an' folks were gangin' away, he inquired how much he had to pay. "Why, nowt," he was told. "So I clicked hod o' me gret club stick, an' went whistlin' oot again." Compare this with the much harsher utterance of Joseph, the servant in *Wuthering Heights*, in the far west. "Whet are ye for?" he shouted. "T'maister's dahn i' t'fowld. Goa rahned by th'end ut' laith [barn], if yah went tuh spake tull him."

Dialect was being spoken by the bulk of the population at the time of the Brontes.

In the West Riding, many regular publications – annuals and almanacks – fixed the character of local communities. The publications were cheap, lively and with a pawky humour that appealed to the grey mass of the people. John Hartley's poems were among those that kept Yorkshire folk laughing in late Victorian times when, as a consequence of the greater literacy that came about through Education Act, the public demanded more written work. Dialect writing thrived. John Wright, of Windhill, Shipley, a serious student of Yorkshire dialects, began his working life in a local quarry, aged six, yet by dint of considerable study he became Professor of Comparative Philology at Oxford. Using material assembled by Professor Skeat, he published (at his own expense) the six-volume *English Dialect Dictionary*.

Music halls became centres of popular culture and accentuated a regional appeal. The fictitious Yorkshire

Tyke was created. The name came unflatteringly from the Old Norse *tik*, a reference to a small dog – a cur of indeterminate breed. The Tyke, dowdy, cloth-capped and mufflered, was partial to smoking and boozing.

F A Carter wrote that West Riding dialect was unequalled as a vehicle for abuse and for threats of violence. *Thoo gurt feeal*, from the agricultural East, meant much the same as *tha gre't fooil* but somehow didn't sound quite so scathing, especially said in the slow East Riding way. Carter added: "When you reflect that in the West Riding you can be *poised, nawped, brayed, fullocked, bencilled, clawked* or *yer'oiled*, it doesn't sound at all a good place to live in. Whilst *claat'eead, blether'eead. cawf'eead, nuppit, baatwit* and *gobslotch* are only a selection of the epithets that can be hurled at anyone who seems to deserve them."

Yorkshire folk-speech has been witty rather than contrived. Though droll it is often humorous, with an element of self-mockery.

YORKSHIRE TYPES

DIALECT helps to bind together a people gravely affected by local government reorganisation in 1974, when Yorkshire, re-shaped to suit the new bureaucracy, lost chunks of its historic territory. Arnold Kellett asserted that despite what appears on modern maps and envelopes, underneath this superficial labelling there is still the original Yorkshire, with the unifying common language of its dialect. Dr W E Sangster, when Methodist minister at Leeds, was an off-comer who earned considerable respect from his flock. One of his flock, moved by a stirring sermon, told him: "Thou'd hev made a champion Yorkshireman."

Dialect has pith and point, as in the saying: "Where there's muck, there's brass." And one still occasionally hears the classic: "Them at hez nowt is nowt – if they'd bin owt they'd hev 'ad summat." A woman living in the north-east was said to be "as thin as a lahtle bit of soap after a lang day's washin'." The best of dialect was marked by a vivid imagery, as illustrated by the comment of a hungry man who "licked a clean thible" (wooden spoon used for porridge) and the lad whose hair was sticking up to such an extent he was said to be calf-licked.

H L Gee, in his little book *Yorkshire Wit and Humour*, contrasted several types of Yorkshireman – the farmer on the Pennines, the inshore fisherman in his coble and the farm man of the East Riding, with its parish-sized fields. Many more Yorkshire types might be mentioned. Charles Dickens, in *Nicholas Nickleby*, opted for the strong but compassionate John Browdie as a prime example of Yorkshireness.

The West Riding tycoon pictured by J B Priestley was inclined to be brash, boastful and at times positively vulgar. In the West Riding of Priestley, bluntness was listed among the virtues. When an admirer of Priestley's work thought his *Angel Pavement* the most wonderful book ever written, Priestley is said to have scowled and snapped: "And what's wrong with *The Good Companions*?"

Dialect, like life itself, is changeful. Sometimes, alas, it is downright sloppy, as in a mill-town where two girls conversing at a bus stop might have been brought up in China. One asked: "Whowoshewi?" (which translated is "who was she with"). The reply was: "Sheworwiahsue." (she was with Our Sue). The running together of words is, indeed, common in Yorkshire speech, as in "Weerstabin?" (Where have you been?).

W J Halliday, an authority on Yorkshire dialect, recorded two good examples of Yorkshire speech: (1) A gooid way to stop a chap's mouth is to keep yer awn shut. (2) A chap 'at's liberal wi' advice is generally niggardly wi' brass.

Dialect waned, being discouraged by school-teachers and largely supplanted by a standard, middle-class speech heard on the radio from the 1920s. The coming of "talkies" to the cinema began the Americanisation of everyday speech.

A SMATTERING OF DIALECT

WAY back in 1900, Canon Atkinson, that grand old man of Yorkshire folk history, deplored "the decay of the pure old Yorkshire speech..." During the many years I edited *The Dalesman*, many readers were passionate about it and were fond of quoting examples. An example of a dry comment that is funny was told by H L Gee. A Yorkshire businessman staying at a London hotel went to the cloakroom for his hat but could not find it. When he complained, the manager launched into a long-winded apology. Said the Yorkshireman: "Appen so. But I'm still baht 'at."

In some *Dalesman* articles, and in humorous stories, I would use a smattering of old dialect words to convey the Yorkshire spirit. A ninety-year-old said of her devoted daughter: "Aye, Martha's a good lass. Ah doan't knaw what I'll do when t'Lord sees fit to tak 'er." A despairing millworker remarked: "If I 'adn't laughed mi 'ead off, I'd hev drowned missen." The practical side of the Yorkshireman has often been commented on. At Sowerby Bridge, it was said: "Doan't believe all tha sees – fathom it!"

Two *Dalesman* characters – Old Amos and Young Fred – conveyed dialect of a sort. Amos was noted for his pithy remarks, such as "tha can't tak thi brass wi thi when tha goes cos it goes afore thou does." Young Fred, sustained by Will Clemence, a West Riding man with a good ear for dialect, expressed his thoughts in verse. We lost a regular reader because of an expression used by Young Fred. The reader complained that her small son, a fan of Fred, often emulated him by saying "flipping heck."

Contributing to the first issue of *The Dalesman*, in April, 1939, Ella Pontefract gave several illustrations of the vividness of expression owing much to dialect. A dalesman said of a small boy: "He were nobbut a peeat high." A man with a high-lying farm noted: "If there's another Noah's flood, there won't be manny people left alive i' England when t'watter comes blashin' down oor chimney pots." A daleswoman said to a camper, who was about to put up a tent: "Tha's niver gaen to lig under yon' lump o' clout."

A FUNNY COUNTY

Yorkshire motto

> 'Ear all, see all, say nowt;
>
> Eit all, sup all, pay nowt;
>
> An' if ivver tha does owt for nowt –
>
> Do it fer thissen!

On the Coat of Arms

> A fly will tipple with anybody, so will a
> Yorkshireman;
>
> A flea will bite anybody, so will a
> Yorkshireman;
>
> A magpie will chatter with anybody, so will a
> Yorkshireman;
>
> And a flitch of bacon is never good for
> anything till it's been hanged…
>
> No more a Yorkshireman.

Tyke. A dog, usually a cur. Also the
comic name of a Yorkshireman.

Grace

> We thank thee Lord for what we've getten;
>
> If there'd been more to eit
>
> There'd have been more 'etten.

Toast

> 'Ere's tiv me an' mi wife's husband –
>
> Nut forgitting missen.

SOME YORKSHIRE SPEYKS

J R GREGSON was born to a frugal life in a West Riding milltown, had a succession of medial jobs but eventually became a noted dramatist and broadcaster. He made his first wireless broadcast in 1924. An avid collector of local folk-speech, Gregson told me of overhearing the driver of a coal cart bawling enquiries about the condition of an ailing acquaintance: "Has he gotten agate o' getting' aht o' bed yet?" Which Gregson described as "a lovely gaggle of g's."

He heard a gossip talking about "Lady Jane Tape wi' edging on." This related to a "jumped up" person she could not abide. Lady Jane was too nice to skin onions and was "one o' that soort that gooas lookin' for lice i' bald heads." A person who inherited a large sum of money when he was too old and infirm to enjoy it was told: "God's takken away thi teeth – then given thi some nuts." His favourite notebook entry was a quotation from an old dame who was giving some advice to a young "over-fond" bride: "Niver put thi husband on a pedestal. He'll nobbut want dusting."

From J R Gregson's notebook:

As fair an' as false as a new gravestooan.

Ah can read him better nor big print.

He'll simmer quietly now he's lettern t'lid off!

He's as much life in him as a bit o' burnt leather.

As uneasy as a dog wi' too monny fleas.

He's a neck like a plucked hen.

If thou wants to play hell, there's no place for a referee.

A further selection:

I wouldn't heng a cat on his word.

Wheer there's muck there's brass.

Her tongue wegged like a lamb's tail.

She looks like a yard o' pump-watter.

Her eyes stuck out like chapel hat-pegs.

Talk about hard-faced; you could straighten nails on his.

He's that well off, he's bow-legged wi' brass.

Sha's warna a hen for pickin' bits up.

He's so mean, he'd nip a currant in two.

A gooid way to stop a chap's mouth is to keep your own shut.

A chap 'at knows nowt – doubts nowt.

Misfortunes come baht seekin' 'em.

Folk 'at think t'least, talk t'most.

Hardest wark is doin' nowt.

Ta mich o' owt is gooed for nowt.

Shippon or **byre**. An outbuilding used for cattle.

AN ASSORTMENT OF SIMILIES

As daft as a brush [stupid]

As black as coil [coal]

As red as a hep [hip]

As thin as a lat [lath]

As proud as a mawk [maggot] in a cheese

As thin as a bar o'soap after a lang day's weshin'

As lazy as a stee [ladder]

As druffen [drunk] as a wheel-'eeard [hub]

As fierce as a fell tup

As blinnd [blind] as a buzzard [moth]

As dry as a lime-burner's clog

As brant [steep] as a 'oose-side [side of a house]

As handy as t'dish clout

As bright as a button [Sunday silver button]

As flat as a bakst'n [bakestone]

As rahnd as a taw [marble]

As wick as a scopprill [spinning-top]

As green as a gesslin' [young goose]

As fierce as a ratten [rat]

As flaysome as sin

As fit as a fiddle

As reyt as a clock

MYTHICAL CELEBRITIES

THE women of Yorkshire were indomitable. Anyone who was ceaselessly busy – "like an old hen that's got off her eggs and on to t'straw" – was said to be **as throng as Throp's wife**, who "were that throng shoo hanged hersen wi' t'dishclaht."

Another comic character, **Tom Pepper**, "was turned out of hell twice before breakfast for lying."

The querulous child was said to be **as queer as Dick's hatband**. A small girl thought it was Dick Satband until she heard the concluding part of the saying "...that went nine times round and then wouldn't tie."

DALE AND FELL

HALLIWELL Sutcliffe, an author who spent his best years at Linton-in-Craven, referred to the fell country of the Pennine Dales as being "where the lean lands rake the sky." In the expressive language of the dalesfolk themselves, it's the land lying "on t'tops". The wind brushes *yakkers* [acres] of heather, *sieves* [rushes] and *Nardus stricta*, that tussocky stuff that trips up the walker. A man would have to be *wrang in his 'eeard* to live on t'tops, but the ground is populated by hardy *moorgam* [red grouse], sheep and walkers.

F W Moorman loved the "tops" and gave us a Wharfedale Lullaby that began:

> *There's a storm brewin' out on Beamsley Beacon,*
> *Thunner an' leetnin' round Simon Seat.*
> *Up amang t'clouds ride prior, priest an' deacon,*
> *T'monks hunt ghosts o' red deer to-neet.*
> *Whist thee, my fair,*
> *Lullaby, Mary;*
> *Bolton's brown monks wean't harm thee, my*
> *sweet.*

Bield or **staggarth**. A short length of wall built
to provide shelter for livestock.

Barf. A long hill.

Beck. Stream.

Brant. Steep.

Breckins. Bracken.

Breea. Hill end.

Carr. A marsh.

Clint. Rock shelf.

Cloise. Enclosure.

Dub. Pool.

Foss. Waterfall.

Gill. Water-carved ravine.

How. Round Hill.

Lonnin. Lane.

Lund. A small wood.

Moss. Peat bog.

Nab. Hill end.

Riddin. Clearing.

Rigg. A hilltop.

-scale. Shed in a grazing ground.

Scawpy. Stony.

Scrog. Rough ground.

Slack. A hollow.

Smout. Hole in wall for rabbits.

Stang. High Hill.

Swang. Bog.

Sype. Drain.

Thirl. Hole in wall for sheep.

-thorp. Outlying farmstead or settlement.

Trod. Footpath.

Truff. Through-stone in drystone wall.

Thwaite. Clearing.

WILD NATURE

AMONG the Norse-derived dialect words for birds and beasts are *tewit* for lapwing; *dunnock* for hedgesparrow; *ruddock* for robin; and *laverock* for skylark. A cuckoo was *gaukr* and a hawk *gledr*. The Norsefolk knew the squirrel, that could once *scamper* across country without leaving trees, as *ikorno*. As a boy in Craven, Tom Hey knew the chaffinch as the *piefinch* – why, he could not imagine – and the starling invariably was the *Shepster* [sheep stare]. A verger at a Dales parish told the vicar who was welcoming parishioners at the church door: "The Shepsters are coming in, sir." He was instructed by the vicar to show them to their pew. The magpie was *nanpie* and said to chatter wi' owt or wi' nowt."

Here are some more rural terms:

    Attercrop. Spider.

    'Aigs. Haws.

    Birk. Birch.

Bleeberry. Bilberry.

Bummel-kites, blegs. Blackberries.

Cleat. Coltsfoot.

Cleg. Horse-fly.

Crake. Crow.

Furze. Gorse.

Gowk. Cuckoo.

Hullet. Owl.

Moorcock. Red grouse.

Moorpoot. Young grouse.

Moss-crop. Cotton grass.

Mowdywarp. Mole.

Teeafit or tewit. Lapwing.

Twitchbell. Earwig.

Urchin. Hedgehog.

Yacker. Acre.

Varmint. Vermin.

Wurrum. Worm.

Yak. Oak.

WEATHER LORE

I N a region of low horizons, the sky seems to occupy two-thirds of the view. Often, it's mucky and *ossin' to slart* [starting to rain] or *tewtlin* [beginning to snow]. Eventually it will *tak up* [brighten]. Everything is revealed with clarity and colour. On Greenhow Hill, over 1,200 ft above sea level, the wind is of the lazy variety, determined to go through a person rather than taking the trouble to go round. A hillman told the author: "Wind's that strong on Greenhow it nearly blows thi 'ead off." In a rainless springtime, the softer moorland vegetation *snirkles* [shrivels].

> **Brimmin.** Misty as snow thaws.
> **Clashy.** Stormy and wet.
> **Dazzened.** Cold, starved.
> **Floudby.** Cold and wild.
> **Glave.** Shiveringly cold.
> **Glisky or glishy.** Too bright too early.

Glockenin. Start of thaw.

Gussy. Growy.

Hime. Hoar frost.

Packy. Cloudy.

Roke. Drizzly.

Siling. Raining heavily.

Slape. Slippery.

Snaw-broth. Melting snow.

Snizy. Damp and cold.

Stourin or dusslin. Driving snow.

Thunder pash. Unexpected shower.

Reeasted. A horse that refuses to go.

THE FARMING SCENE

D IALECT once formed a high proportion of a
Dales farmer's speech. A test-piece for off-
comers was to understanding the question – "Ast
ivver lugged 'ool up a stee till thi rig warked?"
(Answer: Have you ever carried wool up a ladder until
your back ached?).

When I – a townie – began courting a Dales
farmer's daughter, haytime was in progress. My task
was *pikin' t'dyke*, which involved taking a wooden fork
and cleaning out dyke-bottoms, a task soon to be
relegated to the history books. The fork was also
employed to *kem t'cart*, this being the process of
removing loose strands of hay from a horse-drawn
cart before it began its journey to the barn.

The old English scythe – the type used for mowing
fields – was a *ley* or *long pole*, its blade properly *laid in*
at the right angle for a specific person. A four-sided
piece of wood known as a *strickle*, and used for sharpening, was attached to the shaft and maintained the

scythe's balance. Haytime terms included *strawing* or *tedding* [spreading out hay for quicker drying] and *footcock* [a forkful of hay, made temporarily weather-proof]. Next in size were a *hub*, composed of grass that was almost hay, and, largest of all, a *pike*.

In Swaledale, a farmer remarked: *Ah nivver count ma sheep. Ah ken ivvery yan i' t'flock.* He was often a solitary figure in the landscape, with dog at heel, but yance a week he would attend the weekly market with his fellows, all representing a fellside culture – small-time and self-reliant. A hill farmer was inclined to put the interests of his sheep before those of his wife, saying: "If owt happened to me, t'wife could cope. My sheep depend on me." He was usually referred to as *maister, boss* or *gaffer*. His wife was *missus*. A farmer who was financially insecure, when asked how he was, replied: *Ah's aw reight – i' health.* He would then confess to be *hoppin' fra twig to twig.*

Muck-spreading, with dung from the shippons, put new life into jaded pastures. It had specialist tools, one of which was a *muck-drag* (for dragging firm muck off the cart). Softer muck was dealt with using a *kow-rake*, *kow* being a term for "pulling anything about". At the outbuildings, there was a *provin bucket*, with straight sides, for feeding stuffs and a *cawf* or calf bucket, which came in various sizes and had tapered sides or what some would call a pail.

Some farming terms:

Balk or Bawk. Loft created by boarding over shippon in a barn.

Band. Rope.

Barfin or braffan. Horse collar.

Beastins. First flush of milk after calving.

Beeasts. Cattle.

Bink. A stone bench in a farm dairy.

Boose. A stall in a shippon.

Bullstin. Whetstone for scythe.

Cawf. Calf.

Cawkers or Carkers. Clog irons.

Clarts or Claps. Cow dung.

Cock-stride. Short distance.

Coo-oose. Cow byre.

Coop. Cart body on sleds.

Dasher. Appliance for strewing hay.

Dess. A lump of hay.

Duffy. Especially light hay.

Ewe. Female sheep.

Faad. Sheep fold.

Fog. Second flush of grass in a meadow.

Foil. Land that has been trampled.

Footcock or whappcock. A small heap of hay.

Gaivelock. A large crowbar.

Gezling. Gosling.

Gimmer. Young female sheep.

Gist. Summering-out young cattle on another's land.

Gripe. Fork used for shifting dung.

Grupe or greeap. Channel for dung in byre or shippon.

Heafed or heughed. Sheep kept on "stinted" upland.

Heck. Back door of a cart.

Hog. Sheep in its first year.

Hopple. Restrain sheep by tying them together, leg to leg.

Hub. Cube of peat.

Hull. Pig sty.

Jag, jaggin. A small load.

Ked. Sheep louse.

Kist. Large wooden box with hinged lid for storing meal.

Kye. Cattle.

Laithe. Barn.

Lug. Ear. The lug mark on a sheep helps to determine ownership.

Hull. Pig sty.

Jumper. Metal tool for driving holes in stone.

Moor-jock. Moorland sheep.

Muckment. Rubbish.

Peeark. Hen perch.

Piggin. Small bucket.

Poke. Sack. One is advised never to buy a pig in a poke.

Recklin. The weakest in a litter.

Rigged. A sheep on its back that is unable to turn.

Scale. The act of spreading manure.

Settlestins. Stones on which cows lie in byre or shippon.

Shelvins. Extensions to cart body to increase its carrying capacity.

Shippon. Cow-shed.

Skep. Agricultural basket.

Snagger. Chopper for removing the tops of turnips.

Spain. Wean.

Spurlins. Cart ruts.

Stag. A yearling colt.

Stee. Ladder.

Stiddy. Anvil.

Stint. Pasturage of a sheep on a moor where grazing is strictly regulated.

Stirk. Yearling bull or heifer.

Strickle. Wooden implement for sharpening scythe.

Swape. The handle of a grindstone.

Swiddening, swizzening. Selective moor-burns to encourage growth of new heather shoots.

Tentin. The care of stock being grazed at road-side.

Tup. Male sheep.

Wether. Castrated lamb.

Whittle. Short-bladed knife used by a butcher.

Wye. A heifer.

Yow. Ewe.

Sward'l. Swaledale sheep, a type that was originally bred on and around Tan Hill.

In the Home

IN great-grandmother's day, life was labour-intensive – and uncomfortable. A cold water tap was connected to the kitchen *slopston* [sink], pans were made of cast iron and clothes were washed with the help of a *peggy-stick*. Lighting was provided by candle or oil-lamp. Sanitation involved journeys in all weathers to a *privy* [toilet], which was a rose-embowered edifice at the bottom of the garden.

The living-room was usually called *house* because it was here the family spent most of their time. It was, in effect, a working kitchen with a wide, tall, iron fireplace, the ledge at the top flanked by pot dogs. The fireplace's immaculate appearance was maintained by a weekly application of black-lead. The decorative piece of ironwork that kept the ashes out of sight was known as a *tidy betty*.

In Swaledale, if you poked the fire hard it was known as *chorring*. Whether peat or coal fuelled the fire, the housewife liked it to be *lowin nicely* which meant it was burning smoothly, without fuss and without too much smoke. A smoking fire was *reeking*. Peat left a fine white dust everywhere. Coal, especially the thin, hard, slaty stuff mined in the Yoredale series of rocks, put down more *seeat* [soot]. On one side of the fireplace was a boiler and on the other the *yuvvin* or *yivvin*, as the oven was called. Any *starved* [chilled] member of the family sat on a fireside stool, known as a *crocket* or *cowpie*.

In the *shaymer* [bedroom], a few mats covered the *fleear* [floor]. The bed, with a mattress made of feather or flock, was covered by a *twilt* [quilt].

Appin. Bedclothes.

Beases. Pillow cases.

Brat. Apron or pinafore.

Buffet. Stool.

Creeaks. Hooks.

Crudds. Curds.

Deg or Dag. Dampen with water.

Donkey or Maiden. Clothes-horse.

Flish. A blister.

Foisty. Damp, musty.

Hastin. Hearth.

Kitlin. A kitten.

Neeak. Inglenook.

Privy. Earth closet.

Piggin. Lading can.

Plenishin. Furniture.

Reach to. Help yourself.

Rench. To rinse.

Sile. To sieve.

Snap. Snack.

Sneck. Door latch.

Voider. Clothes basket.

Winterhedge. Clothes horse.

Wishen, Wishin. Cushion.

FOOD AND DRINK

A YORKSHIREMAN'S heart was said to be like Yorkshire Pudding – crisp outside but soft within. It was crisp outside because the pudding mixture was plunged into fat contained in a rectangular dripping plan. The fat was so hot it smoked. You were offered Yorkshire pudding at the start of the meal – usually the Sunday meal. Pudding was popular in frugal times as a cheap belly-filler; hence the saying – *Them 'at eyts mooast puddin' gets mooast meat.* Most likely, the meat was a lump of beef.

Not all farmhouse fare was as toothsome as we have been led to believe. A farm man described some particularly hard pastry as "that hard tha could shoe hosses wi' it." He added: "I reckon there's lots o' first-rate jock-shops – but mine were never among 'em… And I was allus a good trougher." Farms with a poor reputation for catering became well-known. A farm labourer might say of a particular place: "If tha goes theer, tha'll get nowt to eat."

Much more favourable was the food set before another farm man who, asked to say grace, observed: "God bless us all, an' make us able/To eat all t'stuff 'at's on this table." The diet tended to be tedious and starchy. A man who lived at the dalehead found himself yearning for the fish and chips people told him about. At long last, he was able to visit a fish and chip shop and sample them. The prospect was alluring. He put a chip in his mouth, chewed for a moment or two, spat it out and said: "It's nobbut a tatie."

The living kitchen of a farm had a deal table and flanking forms, with perhaps a good wooden chair at the head of the table for the farmer to use. At breakfast time, porridge and bacon were served. The porridge was stirred by a piece of wood known as a *thible*. A chest in which oatmeal was kept was known as an *oatmeal kist*. It was of rough construction, pegged together rather than being nailed.

The ultra-rich first flush of milk produced by the cow for its calf for several days after calving was known as *beastings*. It might be as thick and yellow as custard with traces of blood in it. A farmer's wife used it to make a pudding.

Allicar. Vinegar.

Bakst'n. Flat stone, heated from beneath, on which oatcake was baked.

Bait. A packed lunch.

Barm. Yeast.

Brussen. Burst, distended with over-eating.

Bread fleake. Overhead rack.

Cat-lap. Weak tea.

Cramming. Stuffing a pig with food to improve its weight.

Fleeak. Rack suspended just below ceiling for drying oatcake or clothes.

Gulla. Oatmeal porridge.

Havercake. Oatcake.

Jacob's Join. Communal tea.

Jock. Food.

Parpin. Salt.

Pobbies. Bread in milk.

Poddish. Porridge.

Reesty. Rancid.

Sleck. To put out a fire.

Snap. Snack.

Spice. Sweets.

Taffled. Tangled.

Tonnup. Turnip.

Wame. Belly.

Wig. Cake with currants.

Fleeak or **Fleg**. Wooden rack for drying oatcake
and clothes.

HUMAN AFFAIRS

IT has been said that a level-headed Yorkshireman is a chap wi' a chip on each shoulder. Dalesfolk are clannish, though not as bad as t'Scots. We don't go to the extent of wearing kilts. The down-to-earthness of Dalesfolk was illustrated by the local preacher who, having told the story of the Prodigal Son, ended it dramatically, flinging out his words and saying in a loud voice: "And soa t'lad came 'ooame agean. And 'e wor clarted up wi' pig-muck." A dalesman gives the impression of being sentimental at times. Soon after the arrival of a first baby, the proud father, a farmer, broke off from the unending business of makkin' brass and was seen standing by the cot, gazing intently into it. His wife approached, tears welling in her eyes, and offered the proverbial penny for her husband's thoughts. He replied: "Nay lass – I think we paid too much for yon cot."

Women didn't dress for show. In the days of bustles and flounces, a hard-up farmer's wife told her dress-maker: "I want summat plain – not puckered up at t'backside." Biblical names for people were commonplace. A distant relative of the author, who had the ill-luck to be christened Hobodiah, was widely known as Our 'Ob.

Amang-hands. An intermediate job.

Baatwit. Witless or stupid.

Bairn. Child.

Bamsey. Fat, red-faced woman.

Belk. To belch.

Bethowt. Remembered.

Blaate. Bashful.

Brass. Money.

Brat. Apron.

Bray. To beat or pound.

Brazzened. Shameless.

Caingy. Bad-tempered.

Cap. To surprise.

Cawf'eead. A silly man.

Claat-eead. Dimwit, Stupid.

Clack. Gossip

Clemmed. Thirsty.

Cowly-handed. Left-handed.

Cowthered. Coddled.

Dother. Shake.

Doy. Endeared.

Dree. Tedious.

Fettle. Mend.

Fizzog. Face.

Flayd. Afraid.

Flish. A blister.

Flit. Remove.

Frame. Undertake something correctly.

Funny-ossity. A quirky person.

Galluses. Braces for trousers.

Gammerstang. A girl of low morals.

Gang. To go.

Gauk-handed. Left-handed.

Gob. The mouth.

Gowk. A fool.

Hig. Take offence.

Kainjie. Peevish.

Kittle. To itch.

Laik. To play.

Lap up. To terminate a job.

Lish. Agile.

Maffly, Faffled. Confused.

Manky. Scruffy.

Marlarking. Larking about.

Near. Stingy.

Pawky. Cheeky.

Sackless. Lazy.

Scrat. Fuss.

Scrow. Muddle.

Seg. Hard skin.

Skellerd. Twisted.

Skitters. Diarrhoea.

Sneevelin. Underhand.

Starved. Cold.

Thoil. Begrudge.

Thropple. Gullet.

Wick. Lively.

Yonderly. Vague.

Not So Weal

DALESFOLK usually managed without doctors. They had their own remedies – including, occasionally, some intended for sheep – and were prepared to "dee naturally". A press photographer who visited a ninety-six year old farmer afterwards said he hoped he would have the pleasure of re-visiting him to take his photo when he had become a centenarian. Said the dalesman: "Tha looks aw reet. Ah doan't see why tha shouldn't."

Men suffer far more than women. At least, that's the impression you get. The farmer's wife struggles through the week with a sprained wrist. Her husband, at the start of a cold, sits by the fire, head in hand, raises his head and gives a window-rattlin' sigh which, if uttered on stage, would be worthy of a medal. One chap who was *sickenin' for summat* told a friend: "This morning, I didn't knaw whether to mak' me bed or get into it." He was in a state known to countless dalesfolk as *fair to middlin'* [depressed]. A

Methodist minister who was summoned to an ailing man's bedside said he had been pleased to call even though they were Anglicans and he would have expected the vicar to be needed. "Nay," said the housewife, "we don't know what my husband's got and we daren't risk our chap."

Stalled – fed up.

Tantling – tottering.

Tewed – over-tired.

Crammelled – stiff-limbed.

Cranks and hods – aches and pains.

Creeas – measles.

Bellowsed – tired.

Crambly – uncomfortable feet.

Dowly – depressed.

Geg-eyed – squint-eyed.

Keggly – unsteady.

Lengelled – harrassed.

Mafted – over-heated.

Mangey – peevish.

Moithered – het up.

Nantling – feeble.

Nithered – shivery cold.

Oinned – harrassed.

Pow-fagged – irritable, overworked.

Colly-wobbles – in a state of nerves.

Run Down – under the weather.

Twined – dissatisfied.

Half-baked or Slack Set Up – jaded

A Poor Colour

Down i' t'Mouth

Clogged up.

Going Back'ards.

Jiggered.

IMPROVING

A MAN who had been "given up" and looked ready to "cross Jordan", as the chapel-folk called the last experience, had a niece who rang up a friend in town and said she might be calling. She told her friend: "Jack's dying and I'll have to buy summat suitable to wear at t'funeral." She did not call. When the friend inquired about it, she was told: "Jack got better."

> Takken a turn.
> Bucking up.
> Bearing up.
> Mending.
> Perked up.

LAST LEGS

AWHEEZY old chap hobbled out of a churchyard after attending a funeral. He encountered one of his pals who said: "There isn't much point thee goin' home, is there?" The widow of a man who had recently died disputed the cost when she asked the local barber to shave him. He wanted to charge half a crown. She said it was too much. "He's not goin' onnywhear special."

A dying man was *piking off* or *tewed out*. He *couldn't hod up*. At the funerals of old, biscuits – like short-bread, flavoured with caraway seeds and stamped with a heart – were handed to the mourners as they arrived at the house. The mourners ate the biscuits and were inclined to keep the wrappers, on which were printed verses from hymns.

Some Dales comments on death:

> *They that wed before they're wise, will die before they thrive.*
>
> *We mun oather owd be – or young dee.*
>
> *We've getten him put sideways (of a burying).*
>
> *A Yorkshireman 'ull push his way through t'pearly gaates while other folk stand an' stare at 'em."*

More Broad Yorksher

Addlings. Wages.
Ale-draper. A publican.
Amell. Between.
Appin. Bed-clothes.
At-after. In a while.
Aud-Lad. The devil.
Awvish. Middlin' in health.

Babbish. Childish.
Backen. Retard.
Badger. A huckster.
Back-o-beyond. Remote.
Bass. Matting.
Bauf. Lusty.
Baxter. A baker.
Beeskep. A straw beehive.
Behint. Behind.
Beholden. Indebted.
Belk. To belch.
Bellywark. Bellyache.
Bide. To lodge or endure.
Blash. Frivolous or nonsensical.
Blate. Bashful.
Blob. A water blister.
Blether. To weep aloud.

Botched. Poorly mended.
Brashy. Inferior.
Bruff. A halo round the moon.

Caggy. Ill-natured.
Canny. Clever.
Carking. Discontented.
Carlings. Grey peas.
Chunter. Murmur.
Clatter. Din.
Cockshut. Close of day.
Collops. Slices of meat.
Cranky. Stiff-jointed.
Cranshy. Gritty.
Cruds. Curds.

Dauby. Untidy.
Deedless. Indolent.
Deft. Neat.
Donk. Damp.
Dowly. Melancholic.
Down in t'Mouth. Dispirited.
Dozzen'd. Shrivelled.
Dreesome. Tedious.
Droppy. Rainy.

Ee. Eye.
Eldin. Kindling.
Elmother. Step-mother.
Ernder. Elevenses.

Fash. Trouble.
Fast. Lacking.
Fendable. A good manager.
Fettle. To mend or adapt.
Flaid. Frightened.
Flaysome. Fearful.
Foil. Trample.

Gaston. High-spirited.
Gawmless. Simple.
Gawk. A fool.
Gloaming. Twilight.
Gob. The mouth.
Gowpen. A handful.

Haggle. To banter.
Handclout. Towel.
Happen. Perhaps.
Hasky. Tough.
Heck. A door.
Heeaf. Haunt.
Hod. Hold.
Hoil. Hole.
Howdy. A midwife.
Howsomivver. Nevertheless.
Huff. To be offended.

Jag. Small load.
Jock. Food.

Keggly. Unsteady.
Kist. Chest.

Laik. Play.
Lap up. Terminate.
Lillilow. Bright flame.
Lingy. Sprightly.
Lop. Flea.
Lowse. Unreliable.
Lowsed. Dismissed.

Maiden. Clothes-horse.
Meadless. Restless.
Minnin-on. Snack.

Natter. Complain.
Nesh. Cold.
Noppy. Head.

Pawky. Cheeky.
Piggin. Lading can.
Poit. Poker.
Possit. Hot drink.

Raffled. Muddled.
Ranty. Excited.
Rive. Tear.
Ruckles. Peat stacks.
Runty. Short-set.

Sam. Pick up.
Sam Hod. Get hold.
Scale. Spread.
Scrat. Fuss.
Scrow. Muddle.
Seet. Sight.
Shiggle. Shuffle.
Side. Tidy away.
Sile. Sieve.
Slap Oile. Roadside puddle.
Slart. Bedaub.
Slate. Rebuke.
Sleak. Lick.
Sneck. Latch.
Spice. Sweets.
Stalled. Fed up.

Taffled. Tangled.
Tallacky. Messy.
Tantling. Tottering.
Theaked. Thatched.
Throng. Busy.

Wark. Ache.
Warm. Scold.
Wick. Agile.
Wishen. Cushion.

TALE END

NOW there's talk of "going into Europe." From the mainland, over a thousand years ago, came the Angles and Danes who gave us many of our dialect words. We are already adopting Continental customs but, in the Dales, old ways die hard. The old tongue endures. At a village shop there was a request for "leeters". The shopkeeper said: "Litres of what?" The caustic response was: "Fireleeters."